Sex Addiction Recovered: The Ultimate Guide to Stop Sex Obsessing: Science of Sex Addiction Revealed

Check Out My Other Books

Porn Addiction Recovered: The Ultimate Guide to Stop Porn Obsessing: Science of Pornography Addiction Revealed by George Klein

Table of Contents

Part I

Getting Started

Introduction

I want to thank you and congratulate you for downloading the book, *Sex Addiction Recovered: The Ultimate Guide to Stop Sex Obsessing: Science of Sex Addiction Revealed.*

Sex Addiction Recovered is your one-stop source for obtaining tools based on research that will allow you to better understand sex addiction, how to recover from sex addiction, and how to maintain recovery. There is hope to become and stay free.

Topics include:

Sex Addiction Defined

The Moment of Realization

The Consequences

Stages of Change

The Addiction Cycle

Sex Addiction and the Brain

Family Dynamics

Breaking Free from Sex Addiction with Evidence-Based Tools

Healthy Sex Maintenance

And more...

This book is the ultimate guide to achieve the quality of life you deserve and break the sex addiction cycle for good.

This is a book for those who have longed to break the sex addiction cycle as well as for those who are in relationships with individuals struggling with sex addiction. This book is based on evidence and is written by a health psychology professional.

This book is not just about breaking the sex addiction cycle. By learning to work through the causes and utilize evidence-based tools, you will feel more centered, more joyous, more confident, and cope better with emotions and life's stressors. There are endless possibilities when you finally break free from sex addiction.

Celebrate the joy of breaking free from sex addiction and maintaining healthy intimacy with *Sex Addiction Recovered*.

Chapter One

What is Sex Addiction?

Sex addiction is a progressive intimacy disorder characterized by compulsive sexual thoughts and acts. Like all addictions, it negatively impacts the individual and the family. Sex addiction is characterized by engaging in persistent sexual acting out behaviors despite negative consequences to self and others. These consequences can include financial problems, health risks (i.e. disease), relationship problems and/or arrest. Approximately six percent (1 out of 17) Americans are sex addicts.

The symptoms of Sex Addiction can include:

- Distress about a pattern of repeated sexual relationships involving a succession of lovers
- Compulsive searching for multiple partners
- Compulsive fixation on an unattainable partner
- Compulsive masturbation
- Compulsive love relationships
- Compulsive sexuality in a relationship
- Extensive use of phone sex, porn, cybersex, or
- Illegal activities like sex with a prostitute

Addictions

It is a myth that you must be using a substance to have an addiction. There are chemical addictions like alcohol and drugs. There are also behavioral addictions like gambling, food addiction, and sex addiction. Both chemical and behavioral addictions result in stimulation of the same area of brain called the reward center of the brain. During drug use, alcohol use, food binges, and sex binges, feel good chemicals are released such as dopamine, serotonin, and adrenaline.

Sex is different from chemical addictions due to the fact that brain will categorize anything sexual 20 percent faster than anything else. Presentation with food and sex can mean a lot. How a person looks smells, feels, etc. can play a major role in sex addiction behaviors. Food and sex addiction are regarded as two of the toughest addictions. One of the reasons they are tough is because people cannot simply stop eating altogether and avoid food and people likely need to continue having sex in life despite the fact that sex addiction was once a problem.

Warning Signs of Sex Addiction for Observers:

You notice your loved one not showing up for work or not caring about work anymore

You notice your loved one not showing up for the relationship

Your loved one is isolating from friends

What Sex Addiction is *not*:

Sex Addiction is *not* poorly researched. There is plenty of definitive research on sex addiction.

Sex Addiction is *not* fun. Many people have the misconception that engaging in sex addiction is highly enjoyable. This is typically not the case due to the fact that the addiction often feels like it has control of a person and the person become dependent on the behaviors to distract from uncomfortable feelings.

Sex Addiction is *not* sexual offending. Sex offending is a legal term and it is defined differently than in clinical terms. Sex offending is simply non-consensual sexual behavior. If someone is not of age to consent to sex that is offending. If someone shows up to someone's window to watch them undress and it is uninvited, that is sex offending. Sex addiction is not sexual offending. In general, sex addicts are not looking to offend, they are looking to feed a void. Most sex addicts do not offend.

Sex addicts are, however, using pornography compulsively, or hooking up with people online. They are sometimes exchanging sex for gifts or money, they are attending sex clubs, they are visiting strip clubs excessively, attending sensual massage parlors, sexting, engaging in virtual sex, or cruising parks for sex, etc. Sex addiction can take many forms. It isn't just about sex. It's about adrenaline rush. It's about distracting from negative emotions and replacing intimacy with intensity.

We often see professionals in treatment. For instance, lawyers, doctors and business owners are often in treatment for sex addiction. Most of all, we see sex addicts living a double life. Fear is a big factor in all addictions and there is a tremendous fear and stress factor when it comes to sex addiction.

A person is not a sex addict simply because he had an affair or he watches porn.

Someone may cheat in their relationship twice a year and that does not necessarily mean they are sex addicted. Someone may be really into being tied up (they have a fetish) and feel disgusted about themselves, however, that does not mean they are necessarily sex addicted. A person may have sex with the same sex once or twice a year and feel at odds with their behavior or sexuality but that also does not mean they are sex addicted. They may simply not like the behavior and wish they could change the behavior.

In order for a person to have an actual sex addiction, there must be consequences and impairment in functioning (i.e. problems in the relationship, financial problems, diseases, problems at work, arrest etc.)

Sexual secrets are those that we typically have the most shame about and they are typically the ones that we are least likely to discuss.

Causes of Sex Addiction:

One of the causes of sex addiction can be neurochemical given the fact that research has shown that antidepressants have been effective in individuals with sex addiction. All disorders are caused by a combination of genetics and environmental variables.

The reward center of the brain communicates that sex is necessary for survival. In sex addicts, the prefrontal cortex (the reasonable part of our brain that makes good decisions) becomes short-circuited and they become more likely to act on impulses. However, with treatment this can be reversed.

During sexual acting out behaviors, a person will experience a sense of euphoria. The addict is typically seeking pleasure or relief to avoid difficult situations and distract from negative emotions. Their actions typically result in guilt, shame, and remorse.

Eighty percent of recovering addicts report having some sort of addiction in their families i.e. binge eating, substance abuse or gambling. Sex addiction is an intimacy disorder. Sex addicts are looking for intimacy and instead of finding intimacy and they are putting other things in the mix that will give them a false sense of intimacy. Sex addicts substitute intimacy for intensity. They may seek pain and pleasure or domination and submission. Sex addiction is not defined by a particular behavior. People who have an affair or even more than one affair could or could not be sex addicted. A person who looks at pornography may be a sex addict or may not.

Short screening tool:

Have you ever engaged in sexual behavior that has hurt you or someone else?

Did you do it again despite the consequences?

Have you tried to stop and you cannot?

Have you made promises to stop but cannot?

Do you see the behavior progressing?

Have the acting out behaviors affected a major area of life i.e. work, relationship, finances, legal problems?

Was there a sex addiction in your family?

Sometimes the only reason a person enters into treatment for sex addiction is because they were caught. This is why it is essential that the spouse or partner urges the sex addict and supports their partner fully in recovery.

Early exposure to pornography is a factor. Finding pornography in your parents' room or friend's house as a child can be a contributing factor. Hardcore pornography can have a tremendous impact on the psyche. Psychological abuse, physical abuse, and/or sexual abuse can be a significant factor. The more the fundamental (black and white the religious beliefs are) the more it has the potential for being a factor.

Being raised with the idea that there is something is wrong with sex or sex is something "We don't talk about" can be contributing factor in sex addiction.

Sex addicts are not likely to say no when they are in the throws of their addiction. The may have lots of hook ups. They may engage in lots of porn. They may live for turning someone on. The need can be so great that they don't know how to stop. Unfortunately, the pursuit of sex and sexual attention has life-changing consequences.

Sex addiction is using sex (sexual thoughts or sexual behaviors) as an escape from uncomfortable feelings.

There's a difference between men and women when it comes to sex addiction. Women oftentimes are much more interested in the romance part of a sexual relationship as well as in the seduction. Their motivation may be feeling sexy or feeling powerful. Sex addicted women often hook up with unattainable men. They tell themselves "This time they'll stay" or "This time they'll love me" or "This time I'll feel special" or "This time I'm taking back the power" and it rarely turns out that way.

Sex addicts often feel lonely, scared, guilty, and lost. However, the only way a sex addict knows to get over these negative feelings is to return to the behavior that's also causing these negative emotions. Dopamine, serotonin, and adrenaline (feel-good chemicals in the brain) allow you to escape feelings that you don't want to confront because of the high-at least for the short-term.

There is a correlation between molestation (sex abuse) during childhood and sex addiction. Sex addicts often experience shame around the abuse and there is shame around the behaviors that come with sex addiction. Oftentimes, individuals who had been abused as children want to take back emotional power and control by acting out sexually. They may say to themselves "I want to take back what I didn't have as a child which is power".

82 percent of sex addicts have been sexually abused. When you're sexually abused, you are used as an object so you begin to connect sex to an object relationship instead of a personal relationship. Most sex addicts are medicating psychological pain.

Many times, sex addicts describe their families as rigid, uncaring, and distant. Sex addicts typically come from dysfunctional families. Some sex addicts assert that they only felt loved as children when they were performing (doing something the parents demanded of them).

As a result, the core belief of a sex addict is often "I am unlovable."

When a sex addict feels there are no outlets for their sexual acting out they feel restless. The intensity of the sex addict behavior allows for disconnection of the self and they want more than anything to disconnect.

If a sex addict does not get recovery they will spiral out of control. They will take more risks and require more partners. Sex addiction inevitably escalates over the years. Most sex addicts feel emotionally and spiritually dead when they are in their addiction.

Addicts have a very high threshold for pain. That can be the reason for why it takes so long to get into recovery.

Sex addiction is characterized by preoccupation, risk taking, escalation, and unmanageability. It's important to remember that in order to have a sex addiction the behavior must be negatively impacting a major area of life. Examples of how the sexual acting out could be negatively affecting functioning could include financial issues, problems at work, relationship problems, health consequences, or arrest.

Questions to ask:

1. Have you ever thought you should cut down your sexual acting out behaviors?

2. Have you ever felt annoyed when people have commented on your sexual behavior?

3. Have you ever felt shame or guilt about your sexual behaviors?

4. Have you ever used sex to avoid feeling low?

5. Is it taking more variety and frequency of sexual and romantic behaviors than before to bring the same excitement or relief?

6. Do you keep secrets about your sexual or romantic activities from those important to you? Do you lead a double life?

Some sex addicts surrender in handcuffs. Some surrender due to an ultimatum by a spouse or partner. Others surrender due to financial or job losses.

Sex addicts can lose hours and even days looking at internet pornography, or driving around to pick up sex workers, or getting ready for a sexual encounter of some sort. Sexual behavior is out of control when you shut your phone off for hours. It's out of control when you feel like a guilty monster when you walk out in the world. It's out of control when the rest of your life is suffering because of the behaviors.

In a full blown sex addiction, you want to stop but you can't stop. You hide in the shadows of your desires and nothing is enough. It's an endless desire for something you don't have or that you want more of and this cycle is characteristic of addiction. You tell yourself "I never want to do that again" and the next hour you are back at it.

Chapter Two

The Consequences and the Moment of Realization

Oftentimes the biggest consequence of the behaviors that come with sex addiction is shame (which is typically the feeling one is trying to escape in the first place).

Many times people will say, "If I'm going to have an addiction it would be a sex addiction". You won't hear a sex addict say that. They know there have been so many consequences to their behaviors and their only wish is to be free from the addiction.

A sex addict typically does not have the tools to say no to a sexual encounter. They may have lots of hook ups, watch porn for hours on end, and live for turning someone on. In those moments, everything goes away and you are all body. You don't' think about it you just do it. Sex addicts spend most of their lives addicted to sex and sexual attention. Sex addiction becomes an all-consuming addiction. They live for the high. They may end up with dangerous people and in dangerous situations. They may end up in hotels, they may engage in public sex, they may ask for no names. They always say yes and an addict often does not know the word no.

The need can be so great that addicts don't know how to stop on their own. Unfortunately, the pursuit of sex and sexual attention has life-changing consequences.

Consequences of sex addiction include loss of time, loss of friends-use sex as a substitute for a close social relationships, loss of work, loss of money, arrest etc. Anything that has any meaning to an addict falls away as a result of the sex addiction.

One of the biggest consequences of sex addiction is the impact on close relationships.

A spouse of a sex addict has to deal with the sudden realization that the partner has been acting out in sex addiction behavior. This is felt and processed as a betrayal. The betrayal could be in the form of watching internet porn, going to prostitutes, going to massage parlors, or having serial affairs. This list is by no means exhaustive. Any behaviors that have been going on in secret and then suddenly come to light are processed by the spouse as betrayal. The partner is undoubtedly going to be in shock and feel betrayed. The partner is confronted with this major betrayal and they are left to deal with it.

Although it is tremendously traumatic for a spouse or partner to learn of their partner's sexual escapades, approximately 80 percent of couples stay together after discovering the sex addiction. Sex addiction is real and it is treatable. When clients sit down in therapy for the first time they usually feel hopeless. What sex addiction counselors want clients to know is that there is hope.

Recognizing that you have sex addiction can be uncomfortable at minimum and frightening at maximum. With all the devastation, depression, and anxiety that sex addiction brings, it is often the wish that they can just flip a switch and turn off the desires for good. However, recovery is a long process.

What can you expect in recovery?

The illusion about sex will come up but it won't have power over you anymore. In recovery, shame will be decreased significantly. Intimacy will be more fulfilling. You will be able to experience real emotional connection with loved ones. You will feel a sense of value and worth. You will be able to form an emotional attachment to the people you care about most. You wil be able to maintain a healthy sex life with your partner. Recovery is long and it can take years but it is worth it. You can never be 100 percent certain that there will not be a relapse. However, after about a year in recovery people can be very solid in relapse prevention.

Chapter Three

Stages of Change

Maybe you've heard that people never change. The truth is that people change all of the time. Change doesn't happen instantaneously for most of us. Behaviors can change but it's not as easy as flipping a light switch. Change comes in stages. The stages of change are pre-contemplation, contemplation, preparation, action, and maintenance. If someone wants to stop acting out in sex addict behaviors, they will go through the following stages.

Pre-contemplation

In pre-contemplation we are typically dominated by denial. Everyone has found themselves in need of behavioral change. Oftentimes, pre-contemplation is brought on by a person near you bringing it up. There might be a behavior that needs to change but the person is not thinking about changing yet. If someone is in the pre-contemplation stage, he/she does not see a problem with their behaviors.

Contemplation

Contemplation is the stage in which a person is thinking about changing but they are not acting on changing the behavior as of yet. There is a realization and an acknowledgement of there being a problem. However, in this stage there can be ambivalence meaning being uncertain if one actually wants to make the change. During this stage, there is some serious thought dedicated to making a change.

Preparation

After considerable thought, one decides to make the change. At this point, a person has entered into the preparation stage. During this stage, a person is taking steps and change will be coming soon. In sex addiction, a person may be researching support groups or therapists, purchasing a filter for their computer to block pornography etc.

Action

This is the stage when the behavioral change takes place. This would be the phase in which a sex addict is abstaining from sexual behaviors. This stage risks the feeling of being overwhelmed. Once an addict realizes what he/she is up against it can be very overwhelming. This is why professional support is so important.

Maintenance

In this stage, behavioral change has taken place. For instance, a sex addict is no longer acting out on sex addict behavior. However, they may be engaging in healthy sexual behaviors with partner. This stage is also marked by managing triggers with relapse prevention techniques. During this stage a person is on track with better resilience to stressors and tools to cope with triggers to act out in behaviors. During this stage, a person avoids places that trigger sexual acting out behavior. During this stage, a person should be attending support groups and seeing a therapist to maintain recovery.

Relapse

This is the stage when sex addict behaviors return. Relapse does not have to happen. However, if it does happen, then the process of stages of change start all over again beginning with pre-contemplation.

As you've read through the stages of change you may have realized which stage you are in at present.

Decisions for Change Worksheet

When we consider changes we don't always consider the pros and cons of the situation. Thinking through the pros and cons of making this change (as well as if we don't make the change) is a way to help us ensure we have fully processed the prospect of the change.

	Pros/Benefits	Cons/Costs
Making a Change		
Not Changing		

Need for Change Assessment

Think about something you want, need, or should be considering changing related to sexual behaviors. Ask yourself the following questions.

Why do I want to make a change?

_____
_____
_____
_____
_____
_____
_____
_____

How will I make this change?

_____
_____
_____
_____
_____
_____
_____
_____
_____
_____
_____
_____
_____

What are some reasons to make this change?

_____
_____
_____
_____
_____

_____

_____

_____

_____

_____

_____

_____

_____

_____

_____

What is your *ideal* outcome when you decide to make this change?

_____

_____

_____

_____

_____

_____

_____

_____

_____

_____

_____

_____

_____

_____

_____

Part II
Inside the Addiction

Chapter Four

The Addiction Cycle and Shame

It is important to assess where a person is in the addiction cycle. This cycle is applicable to any addiction, however, we will be addressing sex addiction specifically below.

Preoccupation

Preoccupation involves thinking about the behavior (thinking about when he's going to have time to go to strip clubs; fantasizing about the sexual act etc.). This preoccupation can last for hours or days.

Ritualization

The ritual is between the preoccupation and the acting out phases. The ritualization is anything one does between thinking about the behavior and acting out on the behavior. For instance, someone might turn on computer to look at porn; drive by a sex club, drink at a bar etc.) Rituals from various addictions can overlap with each other. Drinking or eating could be part of the ritual leading up to sexual acting out. Rituals can be short or long. The ritual could be a few minutes or even a few years. Longer rituals can involve preparing for an affair. For example, people meet online or at a coffee shop and begin to form an affair. Also, a person could be planning a trip to Amsterdam to engage sexually with prostitutes. The ritual would involve booking a flight, looking up brothels etc. Rituals can be short or long depending on the activity.

Part of a ritual is the thought process. What are you doing in your mind that is justifying the behaviors to yourself? Conversations with yourself allow you the freedom to do the sex addict behaviors. If a person is engaged in the ritual it most often leads to the acting out behavior.

As people move closer to the actual acting out they engage in a ritual. It prepares the body to the final culmination of acting out. It becomes much harder to turn back once a person is in the ritualization stage.

Compulsive Behavior (Acting out)

This is when the acting out behavior is occurring. It is the stage in which the problematic behavior is present. This could be going to a massage parlor, visiting a prostitute, going to a porn site, going to a strip club, etc.

Despair

Feelings of guilt and shame are characterized by the fourth phase of the sex addiction cycle. After acting out, the feeling of guilt and shame is the crash. Common feelings that occur during this stage are feeling out of control, self-blame, guilt, and shame. These feelings trigger the cycle to begin over again. Most people with sex addiction feel badly after acting out.

Sex addicts are most likely reenacting arousal patterns from their early childhood trauma, which in turn, further cements those patterns in the brain. The trauma could have been emotional, physical, or sexual abuse. Emotional trauma could look like a mother that was ill and was not available. Physical abuse could have been a father coming home from work and punishing with a belt. Sexual abuse could have taken place during one incident or for a duration of many years.

Story of a Sex Addict's Abuse:

A recovered sex addict once told a story of his physical abuse which he believed played a significant role in causing his sexual compulsivities. Although he was not sexually abused, he found an escape from the fear he had of his father through pornographic magazines and masturbation. His father had been struggling with his own sexual identity issues and repression and would take out his anger and frustration on his children. The sex addict turned to sneaking in Playboy magazines and masturbating for hours on end simply to escape the painful feelings of the physical abuse.

The Connection between Sexual Abuse and Sex Addiction

Sexual abuse can lead to love addiction and/or sex addiction. When awful things happen in childhood (physical, sexual abuse, and neglect) something about that experiences wires our brain into attraction to fear and trauma similar to the trauma. If you had an unavailable father, you may be drawn to an unavailable man. If you had an unavailable mother, you may be drawn to an unavailable woman.

Sexual abuse changes people and their behaviors. Sexual abuse can result in emotional dysregulation and addiction. When you are not yet recovered and you have experienced trauma the trauma is affecting you whether unconsciously or consciously. With female sex addicts who have previously been molested, they typically act out their abuse as adults but this time they are attempting to take back the power with their current sexual partners. The way a sex addict feels they can get rid of this trauma is to self-medicate with such things as sexual acting out behaviors.

It becomes easy to relate to people on a sexual level. Self-esteem is negatively affected and sex becomes one's worth many times. Self-worth issues follow you through life but there is hope.

Chapter Five

Sex Addiction and the Brain

Addiction is about stimulation-plain and simple. Stimulation can come from drugs, alcohol, food, sex and more. What happens when our brain gets stimulated? Dopamine, serotonin, and adrenaline are released in the brain. When we become addicted to a substance or a behavior, our brain tries to maintain a balance (homeostasis) so it begins to shut down feel-good neurochemical receptors. As a result, we need more of the behavior to get as high. Then, when we stop the behavior, normal activities that used to make us feel good are not as pleasurable. This can result in depression and anxiety. It will take approximately six months to get back to the state your brain was in prior to engaging in the sex addiction behaviors so that you can gain pleasure.

Your neurobiology is already altered once you are preoccupied with thoughts of the sexual act. When you are getting ready to act out, your pupils become dilated, hearing becomes more acute, your heart races, and breathing becomes shallow. It's not about the sexual act itself, it is also about everything leading up to the act that takes place.

We all experience excitement and adrenaline rushes, however, for sex addicts, they are able to extend those rushes out. A lot of it is about the excitement. If someone has a gambling addiction, they won't stop when they have spent their children's college tuition. They stop when everything is gone. This is the reason that many sex addicts don't seek treatment until their job or relationship, health, or freedom is in jeopardy.

Sex addiction is the state of consciousness called "being in the bubble" or "being in a trance." Sex addicts will say that they were in a trance when they were on their way or when they were acting out their behaviors. It can feel like they arrived at the sexual acting out environment without knowing it. Adrenaline can allow us to leave the prefrontal lobe (the part of our brains that makes decisions). It can allow us to put us into a much more primitive state. Sex addicts are not thinking clearly when they are in these states.

The areas that are impacted by our unwanted sexual behavior are the nucleus accumbens (which plays a significant role in the cognitive processing of
motivation, pleasure, reward and reinforcement learning), the prefrontal cortex (responsible for decision making), and the amygdala (which process experiences and emotions). If we can begin to understand our bodies when it comes to sex addiction, we can begin to control the behavior. An external stimulus like masturbation is characteristic of a behavioral addiction. Dopamine is the driving force of the high and the addiction.

Many people think that it is as simple as stopping the behavior. Like chemical addictions, behavioral addictions are largely genetic (as in they can run in families). Over time, our brains become accustomed to using sex to relieve emotions like removing stress. We are using the addiction to medicate emotional wounds. Your brain craves the dopamine rush and it results in compulsive acting out. Your brain tricks you into thinking you have to have the sexual act because of the rush your brain is used to receiving.

When a person is reminded of an addiction, we call that a trigger. Sexual triggers occur when the brain registers something through sight, scent, sound, etc. This could be a sex scene in a movie or a conversation that has sexual undertones or overtones. Non-sexual environmental triggers also exist. An example of a non-sexual environmental trigger could be driving by a street because that is the one that led you to the strip club you previously frequented. The street is non-sexual yet it triggers you. A room in your house or an empty house could also be non-sexual environmental triggers.

Another trigger can be an emotional trigger. Loneliness, stress, anger, sadness can be non-sexual emotional triggers. These are the most difficult to understand and to confront. Wherever you are, in whatever place, at work at home, when these emotions occur you want to act out sexually. You may find yourself wanting to act out after a fight with the boss or your partner. Your body is accustomed to act out after feeling the non-sexual emotional triggers. The same thing happens for overeaters. When they experience stress or sadness, they are inclined to binge eat. Emotions connected the behavioral addiction act with the emotion.

Understanding your triggers is critical to change sex addiction behavior.

Take some time on the next page to work through your triggers.

Non-sexual Emotional Triggers

1

2

3

4

5

6

7

8

9

10

Non-sexual Environmental Triggers

1

2

3

4

5

6

7

8

9

10

Chapter Six
Family Dynamics

Families can be sick when there is active addiction in the family. However, when an addict sobers up from addiction it can improve the entire family.

Does sex addiction affect relationships? Definitely does, in fact it will impact virtually all of the people in the person's life. It will affect the partner, children, people at work etc. Even if the partner or spouse does not know about the acting out it will affect them. For instance, a person engaging in sex addict behavior will distance themselves from others. They often feel that no one understands them.

The preoccupation of thought around acting out as well as acting out can take time and concentration from work. Sex addiction can have a very profound effect on personal relationships, family relationships, and work relationships.

True sex addicts do not have the tools to manage the emotions involved in relationships. Many go through several relationships in a short period of time.

Often, family members are angry and stressed and they need to be able to communicate directly with the individual. When a partner discovers their partner's sex addiction behaviors it is processed like a trauma. There is profound betrayal experienced when they have discovered a partner that they have planned their entire lives around has been unfaithful. The partner feels a multitude of emotions ranging from love, hate, anger, sadness. If you are with someone who lies to you, who manipulates you, you are bound to feel these feelings.

The partner or spouse is experiencing something most like post-traumatic stress after the discovery of a partner's sex addict behavior. The partner will experience extreme emotional states (i.e. volatility, lability). The first thing a partner needs to do is realize is that the sex addict partner needs help.

Spouses will say things like "I don't know if anything you say now is true" or "I don't know if I can trust you." Spouses will be hyper-vigilant. They will want to go through the partner's belongings and they may be very irrational. The partner who is in recovery for sex addiction could be ten minutes late and the spouse will be erratic because they are triggered back into that high anxiety state that they experienced about discovering the betrayal in the first place. There is a lot of self-doubt experienced by the spouse of a sex addict. The spouse may have a difficult time disclosing the infidelity of the partner to close friends due to shame. Spouses may ruminate about what they went through with their partner.

The spouse will be in the state of trauma for quite a while. When spouses become intimate again, they can become triggered. They can be reactive and rageful. They need time to grieve. They don't need to be "calmed down." They don't need to look at their part. There is no need to blame the spouse for the sex addict's behavior if the partner is truly sex addicted. The spouses do not do well if they are asked to look at their part especially in the beginning (approximately the first nine months) after discovering the betrayal. They do not need labels like co-dependency for at least for up to a year or more. They do not need to be diagnosed with their own conditions for up to a year or more after discovering their partner's betrayal.

Spouses need time to grieve. They need concrete direction around self-care and talking to family. They need validation of their reality. They need disclosure by partner if they want to hear about the infidelity details. Therapists feel the spouses have a right to know but ideally when they are also in their own individual therapy or in a support group like "Betrayed Women". Betrayed spouses do well in group therapy. They are less inclined to taking their anger out on their spouse and more likely to release the anger in the group therapy setting.

What is the partner to do in this crisis? It is up to the partner or spouse to take the initiative of making an appointment with a therapist who specifically specializes in sex addiction. You can find these therapists on psychologytoday.com and search sex addiction specialists on that site.

Partners of sex addicts must realize that they are in a unique position in the sex addict's life. They are the person with the most leverage. If the spouse or partner is adamant about the partner getting help then the therapist is in a better position to help. It is up to the partner or spouse to use that leverage when the crisis hits to be firm and clear about requirements for treatment.

At that point when the addict is seeking treatment, they often feel like they have been living a double life. It is easy to feel irrational and project fears onto one another. The two partners need to be in therapy separately and together rather than trying to be a support system for each other. At this point, being a therapist to each other is not advised. Support groups, friends, and therapists are to be utilized in the crisis phase.

If the individual struggling with sex addiction has been seen by a certified sex addiction therapist, they may be asked to go to a residential treatment center for sex addiction. They can also go to an intensive outpatient clinic (which allows you to still work). This involves group therapy most of the day typically three days a week. There they are encouraged to be in individual and group therapy. Total sexual abstinence is often recommended at least for the initial stages of recovery. It's usually recommended that the partners not have sex for a couple of months to six months. Sex during the initial stages of recovery can trigger addictive fantasies and hold the person back from having the mind reboot in the way that it needs to in recovery.

Sex addiction isn't just about getting the person to stop the behavior. They could stop doing the behaviors. It's addressing the essential feature of the problem which is an intimacy disorder. What is an intimacy disorder? It's the fact that the person cannot relate with all of themselves in the relationship. They needed to take the most vulnerable part of themselves and protect it and split off. They are intimacy avoidant. The addict has been essentially living in fear of revealing who they are and avoided being open completely with who they are and trusting the person with who they are in a relationship.

Sex addicts often grow up in families where there is an insufficient bond in the parental dynamic. They could have a traumatic childhood or simply emotionally absent parents. Somehow the addict felt abandoned or hurt about people they were closest to so it leaves them in a bad place in terms of forming a relationship.

Building trust takes a long time. Research shows that it takes approximately one year from betrayal for partner to trust. In order for the partner to feel their partner is being honest, they need to see that the addict is in recovery for themselves.

When sex addicts think of intimacy, they think of pain and they think of hurt. Acting out sexually they can feel make the sex addict feel loved in a safe situation by having no strings and by not being vulnerable.

Many people stay together after dealing with sex addiction within the relationship. It is not an option to bring in the family in the treatment process...it is necessary for successful sex addiction recovery. The primary relationships in the sex addict's life need to be repaired. The way that happens is by having the family member or spouse in therapy on their own as well as in family therapy with the person struggling with sex addiction.

In addition to engaging in therapy, the entire family must be meeting each of the eight areas critical to mental health. These include engaging in physical activity, having proper nutrition, engaging in some sort of spirituality, managing stress, engaging in altruism (giving back to others), being involved in enjoyable activities, connecting to nature, and tending to relationships in health ways. These mental health correlates will be discussed later in more depth. It is important to remember that the individual struggling with sex addiction will need his/her family to be in good mental health so that the individual is not so inclined to relapse.

Part III

Action Plan for Recovery for Life

Chapter Seven

Breaking Free with Evidence-Based Tools

One way to change the way you think is by using positive affirmations. Affirmations are sentence-long statements that, when repeated aloud on a daily basis, alter the way you think in turn altering your behavior.

The affirmations on this page have been specially written to **help you overcome your addiction to sex**. It is advised that you repeat them aloud daily and even throughout the day.

I am dedicated to overcoming my addiction to sex

I am free from sex addiction

I am in control of my sexual urges

I am living a life free from sex addiction

I am no longer seeing others as sex objects

It is not easy to say no to my sexual urges

It is easy to say no to others

I am developing strong will power

I have a healthy attitude towards sex

I am taking responsibility for my own actions

I am in control of my own life

I am becoming free of my sex addiction

I will become free of my sexual urges

I am finding myself more positive about overcoming my addiction

I am becoming someone with strong will power

I see people as human beings and not as sexual objects

I am turning into someone who is in control of their own life

I will take responsibility for my own actions

I am having a positive outlook on my future

I have strong self-control that allows me to overcome my addiction

I see people as equals and not as objects

I am not ashamed any longer

People see me as someone who is in control of their own life

Taking control of my sexual urges is something I'm committed to

My attitude towards sex is healthy

I can connect in a deeper way than ever with my partner now that I'm free

I am more centered now that I am free of sex addiction

My attitude towards relationships is positive

Go-to List

There are some days that you will feel triggered to act out on your behaviors. Behavioral modification is a tool we use to change a behavior. We can replace old behaviors with new behaviors. Behavior modification has the potential to be highly adaptive and beneficial from a sex addiction standpoint. Sex addict acting out is a response to something that is triggering you like stress, boredom, frustration, dissatisfaction etc. Set yourself up for success by creating a go-to list when you are feeling triggered. Instead of giving into self-destructive behaviors, you can access this list. Include things like downloading music, relaxing on the sand, finding a new podcast, getting a manicure, or going to a concert.

It has been proven that people who write down their goals are more successful in actually accomplishing their goals.

This is for you...

I'm going to transform my life in the next 66 days (new research shows it actually takes 66 days to break a habit not 28). I already see myself as feeling_____

_____

_____

_____

_____

_____

My reasons for changing are_____

_____

_____and now it's my standard to be a person that_____

_____

_____

_____

_____

_____

_____

_____

_____

One of the major things you must do to break free of sex addiction is to master your habits. We are creatures of habit. We need habits to survive and we cannot function without them. Without habits we would not have successful athletes etc. Bad habits produce underactivity and a bad quality of life. More than 40 percent of the actions people perform are not actual decisions but habits. The habit cycle is critical because you can use the habit cycle to help you bring behaviors that are triggered by the unconscious mind to the conscious mind. To break a habit you must *make* a habit. You must not focus solely on what you don't want to do. You must focus on what you *want* to do. Eat better, sleep better, exercise. Take one small step that will move you forward.

When a therapist asks a sex addict what they do for fun, they typically answer with the sex act (as in "I look at porn" or "I go to sex chat rooms" or "I go to the strip club" or "I go to massage parlors").

Take inventory of all of the things that you used to love to do before falling into addiction. Also take inventory on the next page of all of the things you would love to do.

Activities You Previously Enjoyed

1

2

3

4

5

6

7

Activities You Would Like to Engage in

1

2

3

4

5

6

7

Eight Areas of Lifestyle Changes Critical to Mental Health

1   Exercise

The exercise-mental health connection is impossible to ignore due to the
mounting evidence of the boost exercise brings to people. The new research regarding exercise and mood encourages therapists to do a better job of helping clients integrate exercise into their daily lives and help them to modify their activity regimens. Moving your muscles is exciting because you are utilizing one of the most effective tools for reducing depressive and anxiety symptoms. Even if you aren't currently depressed, you likely experience stress from time to time. In these situations you are likely to experience fight-or-flight sensations (i.e. heavy perspiration and increased heart rate) that may be unpleasant. Exercise can work as a sort of exposure therapy helping you to associate the fight-or-flight symptoms (i.e. heavy perspiration and increased heart rate) with safety instead of danger. This association can help immensely in stressful times.

2   Nutrition

Proper nutrition is shown to have a tremendous positive effect on mood and overall mental health.

3   Connection to Nature

We need some way to re-engage with nature.

4 Relationships

Being in nurturing and healthy relationships is critical to recovery and overall improved mental health. Many times people struggling with sex addiction will have an "800 pound telephone" meaning they have learned to not reach out and handle everything on their own. In recovery, it is critical to be vulnerable and reach out to remain recovered.

5 Recreation and Enjoyable Activities

(These were the activities you listed above).

6 Stress Management

One major way to manage stress is to engage in mindfulness activities. Mindfulness can be expressed in many types of ways. Meditation is a common form of mindfulness. Yoga is another form of mindfulness. Yoga is an optimal way of connecting mind and body.

Mindfulness can take other forms like taking a walk. A mindful walk would involve being aware of the scenery and noticing the scents, noticing the colors, feeling the air hitting your face. Using all of your senses is an important component of mindfulness because it helps you become truly present in the moment. Mindfulness can be practiced anywhere, in any activity, and it can take many forms. It can be practiced while playing a sport, or reading a book, while listening to a guided imagery, or talking to your partner, making love with your partner, or listening to music.

You are fully engaged in the moment when you are practicing mindfulness. You are paying attention to everything in the moment with all of your senses. You are fully present and immersed in the activity. Mindfulness techniques can have a powerful effect on your mood, stress reduction, and it can be used as a coping skill when you are feeling triggered to act out in a sexual behavior. *Remember mindfulness for your go-to list when you are feeling the urge to act out.*

7   Spirituality

Positive Psychology shows us that spiritual practice can increase happiness.

8   Altruism

Self-sacrifice and giving to others is one of the highest correlates to improved mental health. Dedicating time to charitable causes can result in a significant improvement in mood and serve as a positive distraction from acting out behaviors.

Our lifestyles (the things that we do in our day to day lives) have much more to do with our mental health than we typically acknowledge. The formerly noted eight areas that are critical to mental health must be applied for full sex addiction recovery and improved mental health all around.

Exercise Log

This is your workout log. You can use this log to both plan out your workouts and to log what you have accomplished. Note: if the gym is a triggering place for you then you may want to exercise in alternative places such as out in nature or at home.

Monday

_____

_____

_____

Tuesday

_____

_____

_____

Wednesday

_____

_____

_____

Thursday

_____

_____

_____

Friday

_____

_____

_____

Saturday

_____

_____

_____

Sunday

_____

_____

_____

Sex Addiction is not about Sex

Sex addiction is not really about sex. It's the searching, the
fantasizing, the hunting and the acting out to distract from
negative feelings. When you are acting out in sex addiction,
you don't have to worry about being rejected. For instance, a
person seeking out a prostitute is confident that he will not be
rejected and that he is in control of the situation. The person
feels powerful in this position. Sex addicts are people who are
desperate to have their needs met but unwilling to be
vulnerable in a relationship to be fully emotionally satisfied.
They are unable, incapable or unwilling to be open enough to
get their true emotional needs met.

Sex addicts seek intensity versus intimacy. Many people who
feel stressed self-soothe through de-escalation meaning they

seek down time, watch TV etc. However, when sex addicts experience stress or other negative emotions, they seek escalation meaning intense sexual acting out behaviors.

Break Out of the Urge to Act Out

You have a pattern of sitting at your computer desk and scanning porn or social media or dating sites when you are feeling stressed or depressed. What I'm about to teach you will help you break that habit. This technique will help you change your destructive patterns. It's simple and it's a prescription for change.

#1 Get yourself in that destructive state that's making you depressed/anxious/stressed...For example, you have a pattern of sitting around feeling stressed (How would you stand? What would your physiology be like?) Your head may be down. You are focusing on shame or how things never change. Wherever you usually are in your home or wherever you are when you are triggered to act out go there in your home. Say the things that you say to yourself when you're in that state "I feel horrible" "I feel like a loser" "I'm ashamed"... Intensely feel that emotional state. Keep affirming these negative thoughts until your physiology matches (your body is slumped, your head is down...). Whatever you usually say and feel in that state, say and feel it with intensity.

#2 While you are feeling that emotional state, just at the peak of that feeling, do something *explosive* to jolt your nervous system. Shock your nervous system by shouting "Wake up!" Or shout a powerful statement like "Get up!" Shout it out loud and at the same time do something physical...jump up and down or spin around or pound on your chest and grunt-do something hilarious. Do anything to get up and out of the state you were in before. This is an example of pattern interruption.

#3 Now, put yourself in the state that you need to be in to feel grounded. Replace the negativity with something new and empowering. Ground yourself, center yourself, take in deep breath, smile, look up, visualize what you want, focus on your what you want for yourself, get excited about your life and how you want it to look.

You have successfully begun to interrupt the old pattern that was causing you to self-soothe with acting out behaviors. In order to condition yourself positively you must repeat this pattern interruption over and over again. Whenever you find yourself in that negative state (anxious, stressed, frustrated, bored, down) which is causing you urges to act out, break out with your powerful pattern interruption ritual. Condition yourself by repeating it so many times that it becomes habitual. Interrupt the pattern. The new replacement pattern that you've created can have a significant improvement on your quality of life.

Treatment

Behavioral problems require behavioral forms of treatment. This means that treatment for sex addiction should include structure, psycho-education, tasks, and high accountability. Treatment should be gender separate meaning the sex addictions groups should be separated by gender. Groups need to be specific to this issue not simply an addictions group. Problem behaviors need to be contained before real recovery happens. Group work is almost always more effective than individual therapy with sex addicts. This is because group members can catch issues that the facilitator or the therapist may not. Sex addicts need relapse prevention. They should be referred to 12-step support groups or other support groups geared specifically toward sex addiction as well as individual therapists specializing in sex addiction.

What is drug and alcohol sobriety? Abstaining from substances. What is sobriety from sex addiction? It's not abstaining from sex for the rest of your life. Healthy sex maintenance is involved during recovery. The sexual behaviors that need to stop should be written down and agreed upon between you and your partner. Take inventory of what problem behavior is on the following page.

Problem Behavior I Will Abstain From

_____
_____
_____
_____
_____
_____
_____
_____
_____
_____
_____
_____
_____
_____
_____
_____

Now that you have listed and agreed upon the behaviors you will abstain from, it's critical to replace those behaviors with life-affirming activities and purpose.

Chapter Eight

Healthy Sex Maintenance

How can you have healthy sex when you are in sex addiction recovery?

It is important to first identify those addictions that are addictive. What we want to do is be able to have healthy sex in a committed, caring, intimate way with a loving partner. Many people believe that having sex is intimate. However, this is not necessarily the case. Having sex is something between two bodies. It is the mental preparation and attitude we bring to sex that makes it intimate.

Intimacy is about being connected to the person. It is about really being present with your partner. It's about being aware that this person is dear to me, this is the person I love, this is the person I care about, and sex springs from that caring and intimacy when you are having healthy sex in recovery. Real intimacy is about being vulnerable (which is one of the most difficult things for a sex addict).

What we tend to do is put the cart before the horse with sex. We have sex and then say now we have been intimate. However, in reality, we want to be intimate and make sex an expression of that intimacy. So, when you are ready to have sex again, make sure it is with a partner with whom you are committed. Also, make sure you have done enough recovery work that you are ready to be vulnerable and present with your partner. There are many "mindfulness" activities and practices. If you want to increase the connectedness and intimacy during sex, I highly suggest that you research and practice mindfulness for sexual and non-sexual activities with your partner. This practice along with individual and group therapy with sex addictions specialists is a definitive way to healthy sex maintenance in recovery.

Chapter Nine: Relapse Prevention

What is relapse prevention?

Relapse prevention is a systematic method of teaching recovering individuals to recognize relapse warning signs and to prevent returning to unwanted behaviors.

We usually hear about relapse and relapse prevention as it relates to drug and alcohol recovery. However, relapse prevention is an essential concept for sex addiction and sex addiction recovery. Relapse is defined as the process of becoming dysfunctional in recovery, which leads to a return to sexual acting out behaviors. Relapse episodes are usually preceded by a series of clear warning signs. Typically, relapse progresses from stability through a period of progressively increasing distress levels that leads to physical and emotional collapse to relapse into old behaviors.

To understand the warning signs, it is critical to recognize the dynamic interaction between the recovery and relapse processes. Recovery can be described as related processes that unfold in the following ways:

- Abstaining from sex addict behaviors

- Separating from people, places, and objects that promote acting out, and establishing a social network that supports recovery

- Thinking rationally and engaging in positive self-talk like affirmations

- Managing emotions adaptively without resorting to compulsive behavior

- Learning to change addictive thinking patterns that create painful feelings and self-defeating behaviors

- Identifying and altering the mistaken core beliefs about oneself, others, and the world

When people who have had a stable recovery yet begin to relapse, they simply reverse this process. In other words, they

- Have a mistaken belief that causes irrational thoughts

- Begin to return to addictive thinking patterns that cause painful feelings

- Engage in compulsive, self-defeating behaviors as a way to avoid negative feelings

- Seek out situations involving people who act out sexually or people who trigger them to act out

- Find themselves in more pain or distress, thinking less rationally, and not utilizing coping skills

- Find themselves in a situation in which action out seems like a logical escape from their pain, discomfort, or distress

In order to avoid a full relapse in which you've gone days, weeks, or months engaging in binge eating, you can use the following tools for relapse prevention.

Reach Out-Call a supportive and positive friend or call your mentor, coach, or therapist. Attend support groups regularly and see your sex addiction specialist regularly.

Refer back to Toolbox-Use all of the coping skills outlined in this book including your Go-To List and Activities for Self-Care.

Routine-Quickly get back into your productive routine when you fall off.

Reinforcement-Reward yourself daily, weekly, and monthly. Get your hair styled by a professional, go to a concert, or take a trip. *Reward is as important as routine.* Put reward on your calendar to avoid relapse and maintain the lifestyle you want free from sex addiction.

Conclusion

Thank you again for downloading this book.

I hope this book was able to help you understand the steps necessary for successful sex addiction recovery. You are now equipped with evidence-based tools to help you understand sex addiction, cope with sex addiction, recover from sex addiction, and maintain healthy intimacy.

Best wishes to you.

Sex Addiction Resources

SAA

Sex Addicts Anonymous

www.saa-recovery.org

SCA

Sexual Compulsives Anonymous

www.sca-recovery.org

S.L.A.A.

Sex and Love Addicts Anonymous

www.slaafws.org

Center for Healthy Sex

www.thecenterforhealthysex.com

Check Out the Author's Additional Book

Porn Addiction Recovered: The Ultimate Guide to Stop Porn Obsessing: Science of Pornography Addiction Revealed

www.ingramcontent.com/pod-product-compliance
Lightning Source LLC
Chambersburg PA
CBHW070325290526
45791CB00003B/1267